Like Rain Returning Home

꼬리

Kathryn Collison

FUTURECYCLE PRESS
www.futurecycle.org

*Cover artwork, "view of bamboo water pipe on rock during daytime"
from Peakpx.com; author photo by Jake Collison; cover and interior
book design by Diane Kistner; Haboro text and titling*

Library of Congress Control Number: 2018935043

Published by FutureCycle Press
Athens, Georgia, USA

ISBN 978-1-942371-52-6

To my grandparents for sharing their story with me,
to my parents for always supporting me, and to my husband
and my daughter for being the light of my life.

Contents

I.

II.

III.

I.

have you left me to
wonder if your path is swathed
with snow or cherry
blossoms   even in spring I
can smell your scent on my robes

Nagoya to Hawaii, 1953

Pressing her cheek against her infant son's,
she sought his familiar scent—
wanted it to sweep over her
like wind stroking paddies of rice.
She longed for cherry blossoms
to fall on her bare arms.
But she couldn't escape the smell
of sea salt and vomit.

He mewled when the ship bucked;
she passed a hand across his forehead,
over his tuft of black hair.
She saw herself reflected in his green eyes,
his skin as pale and white
as her American husband's.

She could coo to her son, and he'd take comfort.
But she couldn't speak with her husband.
The English words burrs in her mouth.
The rolling waves of her language swaddled her,
but she was leaving those waves behind
with each buck of the ship.

Singing a lullaby to calm her son,
she stood as rigid and hard as bamboo,
rooting her feet to the floor
as though her five-foot frame
could quiet the ocean itself.

Her Treasure Box in the Back of the Closet Behind Old Zoris

A picture of her mother, head tilted,
eyes focused on the unseen.
Her first jade bracelet, now so small
she couldn't even scrape it past her knuckles.
A passport with only one stamp.
A torn swatch from her son's green receiving blanket.
Her mother's recipe for sticky rice.
A ticket from the Nagoya train.
An obi belt worn at her first
Tanabata festival.
A newspaper article folded
into a crane. Tucked down
in its wing, invisible:
Hiroshima.
Two chopsticks.
Her name inked in black
on a faded yellow scroll.

Nuances

She calls fireflies
glowflies. Her tongue stumbles
then latches on the length of the *l,*
wraps itself around the memory
of his hands, his weight:
limbs stretch
to fit and cover,
to own and belong,
moonlight streaked eyes silver
and splattered their bodies
until they were fashioned
in color instead of flesh. Colors
never seen before
that could never again exist:
blue-green-white
with black filigree.
She knows glowflies don't exist,
that the word is wrong,
but fireflies will never
be the right shade.

Thanatos

Her father's eyes:
black against black.
Night opens its unseen mouth.

We can observe only
the effects of dark matter—
the gravitational pull.

His eyes and not his eyes:
explosion of stars.

Marriage and Immigration

She hates the blank page, but loves
the dry pen.
White paper with its unfilled lines
suggests hope in a way
that is more than she can bear.
It swims with explanations unwritten, apologies
not yet accepted.

But the dry pen is an excuse:
it's not her fault.
She didn't suck the pen dry or lap
at black ink like leeching snake venom
from a lover's wound. Though he's her husband,
not her lover.
An American.

She's torn in two:
one side angry, the other relieved.
She thinks her right side is angry,
the hand anticipating use,
and her left grateful for the inkless pen—
didn't she read that veins in the left arm and hand
run closer to the heart?
But she knows she could be wrong:
she's misread her body before.

Origami

He finds scrapped bits of paper, balled-up
and torn fragments,
penned by her hand.
They're like little treasure maps or ancient
religious doctrines littered all over the house.
He finds them in corners, behind books, along
baseboards, on her nightstand.
What hieroglyphic lore
is written on these throw-aways?
He longs for her to tell him why she junks
some carelessly, some in anger (judging from their ripped
and tattered skins), some in what seems like despair:
ones left mostly unmolested, slightly bent
at corners, fluttering wounded
in her room. She must be writing to her family:
reaching across the ocean into Nagoya,
into her father's home.
But these crumbled bits will never be delivered.

Calligraphy

She touches her skin—
fingers to lips, cheeks,
eyelids that arc
in crescent moons.
She dips a brush in red
to cover every inch
of herself she can reach.
Swirls, jabs of the brush
transform her body
into her homeland.

A sun rises over her small breasts,
while Buddha takes up the whole space
of her stomach. Kanji of strength
and tranquility rest on her thighs,
and her forearms bear
mother, daughter, wife.
Bonsai grace her legs, bamboo
grow along the sides of her torso.
Cherry blossoms and fans adorn her ankles.

She saves her face for last—
looking in a mirror, a more colorful
palette in hand, she paints
the American flag.
Hair pulled tightly back, she counts
fifty stars and thirteen perfect stripes.

English Lessons

Her fingers bend
in unfamiliar angles.
She dislikes the letter *b*,
too fat like a distended belly,
but *z* flows
across the page.

A young woman with red-shining hair
at the front of class snaps
for her to pay attention.
The woman keeps calling her Kitty.
Everyone calls her that now.
She doesn't know what it means.
Assumes it's English for Katsuko.

The syllables don't seem to fit
as they drip from unfamiliar lips.
Kitty. Kitty.
She doesn't like the letter *t*:
a sharp line slashed in half,
penetrating paper.

She wants to fill
her stack of white pages
with long *z*'s
and stand at the front
of class repeating

Katsuko, Katsuko,
snapping
for the woman with red hair
to pay attention.

When They Moved from Hawaii to Albuquerque

Her mouth would not obey. Each letter tore
at the soft tissue of her tongue, scraping
past her uvula. They even caught in her husband's throat.
Who had ever heard of such a place: a city too long ago embraced
by Water, palm smoothing stone, or ravaged by rage,
the kind of rape only she could accomplish?
Instead, Wind and Sun
chip and scorch
rock, bone,
paint the desert—
rattlesnake-brown earth, ginger-red stone, speared-yellow chamisa.
Mountains tear the sky, calm only
when Sun turns his face:
Moon in quiet skin orders her husband to bed.
She cloaks the mountains in pink lace, sombering them with the deep
purple of her veins.

Response on Finding Her Husband's Physics Book

If light spears and separates,
flows in waves, drifts in particles.
If we observe and so change the outcome
of momentum.
If we taste sap and mud
as riverwind lashes us to its breast.
If night cuts like a river
from the earth's womb:
blood and muscle
silt and salt.
If fragments from stars and moons
coat skin and hair,
if the solar system falls off orbit,
spins in space, lost and lonely.
If we float in the void:
a speck of life amidst
the source of life.
If the universe collapses.
If light can be reborn.

Synchrony

Pendulums, if started at different times, resynchronize in thirty minutes. A 17th-century Dutch physicist spent hours in front of them. She wonders what he thought as one slowed and the other quickened to meet its mate. Could he feel their pull to one another across the space of his office? Did books and paper, pens and pencils hear the pendulums call—murmured movement, gentle decelerations?

Fireflies synchronize. Thousands in a field blink on and off in perfect rhythm. What light source could ever shine so bright in a millisecond —waves so intense you were blind one moment, and then blind in a different way the next, eyes trying to process after-images, red and yellow burned into retinas? Or is light from a thousand fireflies softer —reflected sunlight on the moon? She imagines their call must be more easily heard than the pendulums, though nobody has ever told her what blinking fireflies sound like, perhaps the crack of electricity from a live wire.

Pedestrians lockstep. When a new footbridge in London was unveiled to the public, they swayed the bridge. That sway furthered the pedestrian sway, a throng of feet lifting and settling in unison. The proof that it was not a natural disaster: the section where people stood still was also still. There, bodies responded to each other in stillness, a sound so loud she imagines that they weren't even able to hear it.

Home

She already knows there are certain types of loneliness
that can never be inked.
Certain types of loneliness waft on tip of tongue,
tickle vocal cords to lay themselves bare—red
and swollen. And the white-bright stars or the wind chimes
hanging from her balcony can't begin to sing
the melody that lacerates her open
so she's nothing more than blood, arteries, and organs
pulsing with the rhythm of a summer night also splaying
itself for her, just her.
And she stands on her balcony praying to what's left of her god,
fat little statues of Buddha with that nirvana-smile,
but she's here now with nothing but a promise
to her husband to leave her past in the past.
And now she's supposed to find comfort
from a man literally splayed and almost dissected
on a wooden cross—
or, rather, a gold cross with delicate inlays, a reminder
on her neck, a gift from her husband on their arrival to a new home.
But, she's not really looking for comfort,
only the tools for her to communicate
the sound her body makes when called to from a distance:
something heard so long ago that the cells in her body remember,
but for just a fraction of a second.
Just enough so she feels the tenor of it, but never the meaning—
never a way to answer the stars, god, or the wind chimes.

Anatomy

He knows about feeling lost even when tethered to someone you love, and how that makes it all the more terrible, this tie that's supposed to connect you to at least one person in a whirlwind of millions. It serves as a bitter contrast to being alone when you're actually alone, when it's expected, but this! This is a mockery of what it means to be alone. Of course, he could never tell her this. She might not feel the same. Or she might. He didn't study English or literature in school; he was better with chemistry and anatomy, the body giving itself over to him in its vast complexities of functioning: chromosomal deletion, allele frequency, gene expression. But, he knows one thing: words have power. Once breath from diaphragm pushes sound from vocal cords and tongue touches teeth and the word is born, there's no aborting it. Words have the peculiar power to alter life but also to drift away unnoticed. That's what makes them dangerous. You never know which it will be. And, then, even if they do drift, they find their way back. It might be like hearing someone call in the distance: your body responds like it always does to stimuli in the environment, even if, in a kind of defense mechanism, it doesn't allow you to process it. The brain cannot consciously attend to all that stimuli—to ground against feet, air on skin, crickets in grass—but it's noted. Your body peels itself open, however slowly and silently, for those sound vibrations, so you can't let just any word escape from your mouth. That's why he can't tell her about feeling so alone even when he's sitting directly across from her at the dinner table. He doesn't know how her body will respond.

On the Patio of the New House in Albuquerque

Children fly kites in the street. The smallest boy in a red cap asks
his pink-coated sister for help while the sky whisks white and blue.
An older boy dives his own kite to the ground when a tree snags its
string. She wonders how many faces are pressed against windows,
watching her watching the children. We think nobody pays attention
when the earth breathes slowly, exhaling light and wind. How alone
we are in our most private moments, a façade like inverted sky in a
pool of water. Sunlight slants across the driveway before covered by a
single cloud. In the moment before light goes, she feels it fade. The
children have left for taller reinforcements to rescue the kite from
bare-boned branches of the tree that will not let go, but must. Their
coats litter the sidewalk like sloughed skin.

II.

blossoms on water
perched on a tree branch the thrush
trills tears from his
naked throat   I reach to him
sleeves slip away baring skin

Admission

When I was twenty-two, I fell in love
for the first time.
I had my heart broken,
but that isn't the point.
The point is that I started to wonder
how she came here
with my grandfather—
trusted love enough to leave.
Did she bear the marks of her father's anger,
body pockmarked by punctuation,
when she met the young American man on base?
Did he wash away her mother's questions
that stained her face red, palming
her cheeks in his hands?
I see her lost in a sea of papers
and words she can't read, applying
for a permission she can't get from her parents.
My grandfather must have relied on his own body
to talk to her, studying skin as Braille, fingers
reading love in each other's flesh when words failed.

I use fragile words to ask them,
and like wind chimes
in only the most gentle
of breezes, she speaks softly.
The stories trip from my grandfather's mouth
in a flurry of autumn.
But the answers I want lie beneath the skin.

Stationed in Nagoya during the Korean War

From Biloxi, Mississippi, he'd met the ocean before—
spent summers clam digging, sucking out their rubbery insides,
swinging a blue plastic bucket.
He scared his siblings with lobster claws, pinching flesh
of their upper arms and legs. He breathed humidity:
heat and moisture slicked his body.
He could read the gulf:
the schedule of tides, the prediction of brewing
storms from that precise rhythm of white caps, the power of a single
wave that glimpses its opportunity and seizes it.
But Nagoya has tsunami alarms. The word tsunami alone moans
from his mouth. He tastes its force: coppery, like blood,
but not as salty.

Fluency

He shook the last match out
of its book into his palm.
Sounds of the crowd pressed
against him, the way all crowd sounds do:
a phrase or two escaping,
but even those mostly indecipherable.
Perhaps he recognized *arigatou*
or *douitashimashite.*

He headed for a magazine stand, saw her:
barely five feet, smiling, hair darker
than even her eyes.
He bought a matchbook,
went back to the base
for his ragged Japanese dictionary.

In the Telling

My grandfather left out what was said.
He didn't remember those first words.
He just ended the story
with the Japanese-English dictionary.

Christmas. My whole family scattered
about the house, chasing the aroma
of sushi, wasabi, turkey, and ham.
He leans against the pool table as he remembers
first seeing her. I follow his eyes as they watch
my grandmother cutting the sushi rolls.
I wonder how he accented the Japanese
in those first stumbling words.
How he pitched his voice when he asked
her to a dance, to dinner, or
to marry him.

She inspects a crumbling piece of sushi, deems it
"ruined" and tosses it to a side plate that won't
make it to the dinner table. My brother snatches
it up and stuffs it into his mouth.
She sees my grandfather and me watching her, offers
up the plate.

They were married three times:
in Japan, then by the Army, at last
in the United States after blessings from a Catholic priest.

I imagine them floating from place to place
like pods from a cottonwood caught by the wind:
drifting puffs of snow.

I take the sushi, rice
sticky on my fingers.
I can taste their story.

A Dance

Light forms into circles
tracing a girl's shoulder
or marrying the shine
of ribbon bars and branch insignia.

Seconds collapse
as each bit of light flees
to new shoulders, arms, cheeks.
Bass bursts through speakers:
burning leaves
and something sweet,
like honey.

Her fingers press
against the doorjamb,
to grip or to give momentum.
Her dress swishes the back
of her knees, sleeves
cling to shoulders.

She finds him
watching her.
Her fingers push
off the doorjamb.

He Teaches Her about Electricity

Zap of the fallen
power line:
over and over,
a saxophone wail.
Orange mates with blue,
white light tongues
black cable.
Clouds and sky surrender
to the rhythm
of current
seeking earth,
arcing to her pale
feet until she feels
the sun like a scream ripped
from her throat.

Women Who Laugh

When moisture leaves our bodies, skin stretched taut
over the edges of bone—air still pushes
through our diaphragms, our cracked lips.

When my grandfather's eyes narrow, English words pulse
out of his mouth faster, faster, an iambic staccato—
my grandmother laughs.

Lips curl, a tickle builds
in throat, then escapes.
The sound becomes real and not just
a captured breath.
It pulls from lungs and trips
over mouth to make itself heard.

When things are the kind of wrong where we've had three hours
of sleep in two days, and driving home at night shadow
people lurk and we slam the brakes to avoid
someone who isn't even there; when all we hear
is the doctor's voice as it splits us down the middle:
kidney failure, paracentesis, hospice—

the women in my family laugh.

A Cold Night's Embrace

Her heart a blue-white lattice
that stills her, ice
crystals in her blood. Breath clings
air in ribbons, frost knit
into night.
Sky bulges with snow—
gray-pink fabric stretched at the seams,
threads snap
one by one.

Tanka on Learning of Her Father's Death

she remembered lit
incense sticks   shrines   smoke bearing
her ancestors' names
obligation to honor:
on: unfulfillable debt

Desert Mountains at Midnight

Silent and black.
Wind ripples desert floor
as a pack of coyotes explore.
Yellow eyes flicker, flash.
One serenades night with his call
while she stays still:
wind-sand scratches her face.

She Thinks of the White Page

A silent evening in her lost garden.
Water in the bamboo fountain
spilling to earth,
seeping to hidden roots.
Torn and bruised kanji.
She scratches her calls
deep into the page's fibers,
then stabs a long black
line through each.
Seeing the violence done,
she tries to hear the fountain
filling and tipping
filling and tipping,
water singing of home.

III.

prayer strips trail behind
in a long ribbon of my
cries   had I known you
would never return I would
have lit your path with my tears

The Festival of the Star-Crossed Lovers

The last she wore her *yukata*,
before the young American man proposed,
was a Tanabata festival:
on the seventh day of the seventh month,
Altair, the ox puller, and Vega, the weaving girl,
were permitted to reunite. They had neglected their duties,
lavished too long on their honeymoon, and the gods grew angry.
Altair banished to one bank of the Milky Way, Vega the other,
the Heavenly River swelled up between them.

Children dressed bamboo trees with wishes:
prayers for love and luck written on red, yellow,
green, white, and black bits of paper,
bamboo branches offered to the sky.
She can taste her favorite sweet-bean treats,
feel the plucking of the *koto* as if its strings
were fibers from her own body.

Now, silk spills from her fingers:
peach and plum floral fans on creamy beige.
Her granddaughter asks how
people fall in love.
With quick, small hands
she pulls and tucks, wraps and ties,
crosses the obi belt tight.
The kimono drips off the child's body,
pooling to the floor.

She tells her about spending too much time
in love, how Altair and Vega were banished.
But without a bamboo branch offering,
she feels the words dry up in her mouth.
She smooths the kimono one last time,
turns the girl so she can see herself in the mirror.
They stare back at themselves, questions
a pendulum ticking back and forth,
the *koto* strummed to infinity.

Firefly Child

Each kanji character has both
sound and meaning—
an ideogram, an idea, a belief
in each stroke of the pen.
There are so many ways to write
her sister's name—over seventy
in fact. Seventy ways to write Keiko.
Her sister's particular combination
means "firefly child."

Female names traditionally end with "ko,"
which means "child" and is sometimes dropped
when the girl comes of age. She never did this.
She thinks now maybe she should have,
become Katsu, so she had some say in it.
But her parents chose each kanji as carefully
as cutting a bonsai branch.
Americans have nicknamed her Kitty.
Her ten-year-old granddaughter tells her
that most times nobody has a say with nicknames.

Assumptions, she understands.
The too-big smile and slow-bobbing head nod,
squinted eyes and brittle tones, she knows
about assumptions people make.
And she thinks now that English speakers have it easy—
letters are taken together
to signify the thing.

The Space Between

black ink spots drizzle on the page
raindrops
on a windshield
when she stares at gaps between
words
eyes at first blurred
then suddenly clear
she sees
a puddle from last night's rain
fingers arcing across black clouds
chopsticks poised in mid-air
her mother's obi belt

running her hand lengthwise
then down
she teases bamboo branches
out of the text
a nightingale from a tree branch
cries sweet and sharp as her own
the noon train to Tokyo
from Nagoya
groaning as it pulls from the station
distant mountains of her childhood
when she and Keiko walked to the ocean
picking cherry blossoms
from each other's hair

she smells lupine

lavender

scarlet sage

from fertile soil

on the page

she traces

herself in

the spaces between

Crane

She's been a citizen for years.
Her grandson is in fifth grade,
and their class is building
a Sadako Sasaki peace memorial
intended for Los Alamos.
She remembers the first time
she saw those cranes on a T-shirt
on the back of a boy.
She was grocery shopping and had just pulled a gallon of milk
from the refrigerator. The boy was begging his mother
for strawberry ice cream.

Holding the milk,
she just stood there and stared—
long past the time the mother and the boy were gone.
She remembers her hand slowly numbing,
not even putting the milk in her basket,
fingers clamped, rigid,
as she thought of those cranes.

Now, the peace memorial is on the news
and her grandson's class
got to meet Peter Jennings.
There are garlands full of thousands
of colored cranes
from all over the world.

She thinks that if she, too, folded
a crane to add to the peace statue,
and made a wish,
she'd have to change the rules
and wish for both one thing
and its opposite.

What's Left Behind

The most horrifying fact of losing someone or something
is that they don't always leave behind traces, or at least not
something that's enough. I understand energy is never
destroyed—only changed or converted—but what good is that?
If I go back to my childhood home and stand where my childhood tree
once was, the tree once many years older than I, will I feel its energy
like a force field flowing around me in just that very spot?
I try to imagine its particles in the air—it must have left some behind
when the chainsaw ripped into its trunk. I try to picture myself coated
by infinitesimal sawdust or bacteria or even white milk blood
that must've poured forth in a microscopic geyser.
But all I see is empty space.
And all I remember is the phone call my mother made
to tell me they were cutting it down,
hearing the chainsaw in the distance.

When my grandmother first went back to Japan,
after years in the United States, longer, in fact,
than she had spent in her native land,
were the cherry blossoms the same?
Were they as white as she remembered them, as sweet- smelling?
She must have walked the streets in some wonder, if only
because the smells of cooking rice and udon noodles
were at an instant recognizable, but also different
in an unaccountable way. I imagine her
sitting in a courtyard, brushing cherry blossoms off

a bench, listening: cicadas chirping, koi flapping their golden
red and white tails, each particle of water splashing
from a fountain, perhaps even a thrush trilling in the distance.

And still I wonder how anyone will ever know she sat there,
or that my mulberry used to shade the entire neighborhood
in summer—its canopy of green protecting us.
Or how my father and I decorated its long branches in winter,
Christmas lights spiraling to the sky.

The Dance of the Machetes

In the Pacific Northwest

Silver glints in the too-bright sun,
clinking as the men toss them under, up, around
their bodies; black boots a bass to keep time;
red bandanas on their heads.
The women arch their arms
high as they dance in and out
of the paths of arcing knives.

But no one else is calling.
No one else is dancing,
afraid to let the wild and ecstatic yell
issue from their vocal cords and carry them
to a place that smells like red and green chile in the fall,
with hot-sun summers and watermelon-pink mountains,
names that roll heavy in your mouth: Albuquerque, Tijeras, Pojoaque,
Tierra Amarilla, Sangre de Cristo, words that can carry you away
hand in hand with the wild call and answer ritual
between dancers and audience where music invades
your body and you move in a frantic rhythm,
joined until everyone is twinned and linked forever.
The call is one of acknowledgement—
recognition of heat and blood and the power
of moving and singing and giving in.

But, no one else is moving.
And now I see they aren't even performing the dance
of the machetes—it's some other dance from some other region

of Mexico and I've forgotten its name, or if I knew it,
it was probably translated by the *ballet folklórico* dancers
in New Mexico. And the dancers now, though skilled,
aren't what I remember from home;
they seem a photographic negative
that hides more than it shows, a colorblindness that
serves only to remind me of what should be or
that I don't even know if what I remember
was ever the truth at all.

Lost

Why must I feel your hands on me when I look
at the back of your truck,
maroon glinting in a shock of blood and heat.
Roar of the engine:
a growl tearing road,
scattering pebbles on pavement.

Don't blood and heat equal passion?
Waves of desire roaring in ears and pulsing in skin?
But, this isn't like that.
My skin is clean, white, untouched and unhandled.
I don't bear the marks of your love because your touch
is gentle, hands soft and comforting. I only feel raw
watching your truck drive five hundred miles away,
thinking of your call later, your voice
too crisscrossed by wires and static to hear
anything but deadened whispers that cling
to the phone in cobwebs.

I feel the five hundred miles before
you've driven them.
Odometer reset at zero
when you fill the gas tank,
screw the cap on, wipe spilled gas from your hands,
though not before it seeps
into a cut on your left forefinger.

I want to feel you like a knife
in my chest, plunged deep
to penetrate sternum.
I want your voice in my ears,
watching you turn
the corner of the street: acres
of time between us.

Scald

I twist the faucet to its red beacon, steam tendrils
my body, blood vessels expand. I wonder if my grandmother
likes hot baths for similar reasons. I'm addicted to that first quick jerk
when my toes touch almost-scalding water,
the slow adjustment
as I submerge.
I crave the intimacy of not just the water, but heat rising
from water: a lover I can feel but can't see, who grips
my throat so he can enter my mouth and lick my lungs.
Are she and I the same in our red-bloomed bodies,
as we watch blood lattice
our legs, thighs, hips, breasts?
Does she lie on the bed after, enveloped
in blankets to make the heat stay, to make it a part of her,
comforted by constriction, heart beating in hips and spine,
yearning only for this kind of closeness to last?

Haiku Lessons

She's read *Kokinshū*
and Bashō, written tanka
and renga and haiku.
But that was long ago.
Now her fingers stretch across
a blank page filled with a storm
of plum blossoms. She can picture
kimono sleeves sliding
along a wooden table, knees bent on
mats, shoes tucked in a corner.
Her words break apart into counted
syllables, each time pushing the limit
of lines and stanza length.
For now her world has grown pregnant
with too many things to say, sunflower bursts.
Still, she wonders where that
green-tea quiet
has gone.

A Setsuwa

As a little girl, she loved ghost stories.
Her mother had given her a collection of folktales,
pages dog-eared and smeared
with dirt and fingerprints. Her favorite:
"The Rooted Corpse."
A young unmarried woman
who spent most days in her sitting room, fell ill
and died. Her family, being poor, didn't have a place
to put her before funeral arrangements.
They left her in the sitting room.
The next day, they unloaded her coffin
to begin funeral rites,
but it was much too light.
They found her in the sitting room.
After returning her body to the coffin,
later that night they found her
back in the room. This time, her corpse stayed
rooted, immovable.
So, they ripped up the floor,
buried her beneath it, and abandoned the house.

Even though the setsuwa never explained
how or why the body rooted itself, she liked to believe
that the room missed its occupant.
That in its longing called to the body
and the body called back. Was it the room that breathed
life into the corpse so it could return

or did the corpse reanimate itself,
so strong was the desire?
She believed it was both,
and imagined what the story left out: reunion.

The woman exhaled contentment
as her flesh rejuvenated, springing back from bone
as soon as she crossed the threshold.
Floor creaked, walls shifted,
comforted by once again being filled.

Sake Sweet

Summer.
Crickets stir night air with song.
Heavy with sake-sweet
fragrances, a warmth slides down
her throat and tingles into her stomach.
She feels Nagoya climb
her ribcage and spread each rung
apart, trying to grip her
slow-beating heart.

Moon Silk

his breath on her cheek
silver light trembles in a
forest of night leaves

Contemplation on the Equinox

Once, she thought she understood
the moon on water:
ripples plucked the surface
in soft notes. She tried to speak
in river tongue, learn to love
like rain returning home.
But in the morning light,
what she remembers
fades into vignettes:
lifting her head to evening,
calling for the moon to see her,
returning silently to her husband's bed.

Acknowledgements

"Marriage and Immigration" first appeared in *New Works Review* (Spring 2006).

"Nagoya to Hawaii, 1953" first appeared in *The Pedestal Magazine* (Thirtieth Issue 2005).

"Response on Finding Her Husband's Physics Book" was inspired by Jane Hirshfield's poem, "If the Rise of the Fish."

Thank you to everyone at FutureCycle Press, especially Diane Kistner and Rachel L. MacAulay. You helped to make this collection the best it could be, and I appreciate your tireless efforts. Thanks to all my family and friends, especially my parents and my husband Jake, who never stopped believing in me and encouraging me. And a big thank you to Jonathan Johnson, my graduate thesis advisor, who helped shape this collection.

About FutureCycle Press

FutureCycle Press is dedicated to publishing lasting English-language poetry books, chapbooks, and anthologies in both print-on-demand and Kindle ebook formats. Founded in 2007 by long-time independent editor/publishers and partners Diane Kistner and Robert S. King, the press incorporated as a nonprofit in 2012. A number of our editors are distinguished poets and writers in their own right, and we have been actively involved in the small press movement going back to the early seventies.

The FutureCycle Poetry Book Prize and honorarium is awarded annually for the best full-length volume of poetry we publish in a calendar year. Introduced in 2013, our Good Works projects are anthologies devoted to issues of universal significance, with all proceeds donated to a related worthy cause. Our Selected Poems series highlights contemporary poets with a substantial body of work to their credit; with this series we strive to resurrect work that has had limited distribution and is now out of print.

We are dedicated to giving all of the authors we publish the care their work deserves, making our catalog of titles the most diverse and distinguished it can be, and paying forward any earnings to fund more great books.

We've learned a few things about independent publishing over the years. We've also evolved a unique, resilient publishing model that allows us to focus mainly on vetting and preserving for posterity poetry collections of exceptional quality without becoming over-whelmed with bookkeeping and mailing, fundraising activities, or taxing editorial and production "bubbles." To find out more about what we are doing, come see us at www.futurecycle.org.

The FutureCycle Poetry Book Prize

All full-length volumes of poetry published by FutureCycle Press in a given calendar year are considered for the annual FutureCycle Poetry Book Prize. This allows us to consider each submission on its own merits, outside of the context of a contest. Too, the judges see the finished book, which will have benefitted from the beautiful book design and strong editorial gloss we are famous for.

The book ranked the best in judging is announced as the prize-winner in the subsequent year. There is no fixed monetary award; instead, the winning poet receives an honorarium of 20% of the total net royalties from all poetry books and chapbooks the press sold online in the year the winning book was published. The winner is also accorded the honor of being on the panel of judges for the next year's competition; all judges receive copies of all contending books to keep for their personal library.